HAL•LEONARD
INSTRUMENTAL
PLAY-ALONG

AUDIO
ACCESS
INCLUDED

PLAYBACK+
Speed • Pitch • Balance • Loop

ALTO SAX

VIDEO GAME MUSIC

Audio arrangements by Peter Deneff

To access audio visit:
**www.halleonard.com/mylibrary**
Enter Code
7096-4263-6747-3013

ISBN 978-1-5400-3602-5

HAL•LEONARD®

Visit Hal Leonard Online at
**www.halleonard.com**

Contact us:
**Hal Leonard**
7777 West Bluemound Road
Milwaukee, WI 53213
Email: info@halleonard.com

In Europe, contact:
**Hal Leonard Europe Limited**
42 Wigmore Street
Marylebone, London, W1U 2RN
Email: info@halleonardeurope.com

In Australia, contact:
**Hal Leonard Australia Pty. Ltd.**
4 Lentara Court
Cheltenham, Victoria, 3192 Australia
Email: info@halleonard.com.au

# ANGRY BIRDS
## Theme

ALTO SAX

By ARI PULKKINEN

**To Coda** ⊕

**D.S. al Coda**

**CODA** ⊕

# ASSASSIN'S CREED III
## Main Title

ALTO SAX

By LORNE BALFE

# ASSASSIN'S CREED REVELATIONS
## Theme

ALTO SAX

By LORNE BALFE

# BATTLEFIELD 1942
## Theme

ALTO SAX

By JOEL ERIKSSON

# CIVILIZATION IV
## Baba Yetu

ALTO SAX

Words and Music by
CHRISTOPHER TIN

# DELTARUNE™
## Don't Forget

ALTO SAX

Words and Music by
TOBY FOX

# ELDER SCROLLS IV: OBLIVION
## Main Theme

ALTO SAX

By JEREMY SOULE

# ELDER SCROLLS V: SKYRIM
## Dragonborn Theme

ALTO SAX

By JEREMY SOULE

# FALLOUT® 4
## Theme

ALTO SAX

Composed by INON ZUR

# FINAL FANTASY VII
## Main Theme

ALTO SAX

By NOBUO UEMATSU

# FULL METAL ALCHEMIST
## Bratja (Brothers)

ALTO SAX

Words and Music by MICHIRU OSHIMA,
SEIJI MIZUSHIMA and TATIANA NAUMOVA

# IL-2 STURMOVIK: BIRDS OF PREY
## Main Theme

ALTO SAX

By JEREMY SOULE

# SPLINTER CELL: CONVICTION

ALTO SAX

Words and Music by KAVEH COHEN
and MICHAEL NIELSEN

# UNDERTALE®
## Megalovania

ALTO SAX

Music by TOBY FOX

# HAL•LEONARD INSTRUMENTAL PLAY-ALONG

Your favorite songs are arranged just for solo instrumentalists with this outstanding series. Each book includes great full-accompaniment play-along audio so you can sound just like a pro!

Check out **halleonard.com** for songlists and more titles!

## 12 Pop Hits
12 songs
| | | | |
|---|---|---|---|
| 00261790 | Flute | 00261795 | Horn |
| 00261791 | Clarinet | 00261796 | Trombone |
| 00261792 | Alto Sax | 00261797 | Violin |
| 00261793 | Tenor Sax | 00261798 | Viola |
| 00261794 | Trumpet | 00261799 | Cello |

## The Very Best of Bach
15 selections
| | | | |
|---|---|---|---|
| 00225371 | Flute | 00225376 | Horn |
| 00225372 | Clarinet | 00225377 | Trombone |
| 00225373 | Alto Sax | 00225378 | Violin |
| 00225374 | Tenor Sax | 00225379 | Viola |
| 00225375 | Trumpet | 00225380 | Cello |

## The Beatles
15 songs
| | | | |
|---|---|---|---|
| 00225330 | Flute | 00225335 | Horn |
| 00225331 | Clarinet | 00225336 | Trombone |
| 00225332 | Alto Sax | 00225337 | Violin |
| 00225333 | Tenor Sax | 00225338 | Viola |
| 00225334 | Trumpet | 00225339 | Cello |

## Chart Hits
12 songs
| | | | |
|---|---|---|---|
| 00146207 | Flute | 00146212 | Horn |
| 00146208 | Clarinet | 00146213 | Trombone |
| 00146209 | Alto Sax | 00146214 | Violin |
| 00146210 | Tenor Sax | 00146211 | Trumpet |
| 00146216 | Cello | | |

## Christmas Songs
12 songs
| | | | |
|---|---|---|---|
| 00146855 | Flute | 00146863 | Horn |
| 00146858 | Clarinet | 00146864 | Trombone |
| 00146859 | Alto Sax | 00146866 | Violin |
| 00146860 | Tenor Sax | 00146867 | Viola |
| 00146862 | Trumpet | 00146868 | Cello |

## Contemporary Broadway
15 songs
| | | | |
|---|---|---|---|
| 00298704 | Flute | 00298709 | Horn |
| 00298705 | Clarinet | 00298710 | Trombone |
| 00298706 | Alto Sax | 00298711 | Violin |
| 00298707 | Tenor Sax | 00298712 | Viola |
| 00298708 | Trumpet | 00298713 | Cello |

## Disney Movie Hits
12 songs
| | | | |
|---|---|---|---|
| 00841420 | Flute | 00841424 | Horn |
| 00841687 | Oboe | 00841425 | Trombone |
| 00841421 | Clarinet | 00841426 | Violin |
| 00841422 | Alto Sax | 00841427 | Viola |
| 00841686 | Tenor Sax | 00841428 | Cello |
| 00841423 | Trumpet | | |

## Disney Solos
12 songs
| | | | |
|---|---|---|---|
| 00841404 | Flute | 00841506 | Oboe |
| 00841406 | Alto Sax | 00841409 | Trumpet |
| 00841407 | Horn | 00841410 | Violin |
| 00841411 | Viola | 00841412 | Cello |
| 00841405 | Clarinet/Tenor Sax | | |
| 00841408 | Trombone/Baritone | | |
| 00841553 | Mallet Percussion | | |

## Dixieland Favorites
15 songs
| | | | |
|---|---|---|---|
| 00268756 | Flute | 0068759 | Trumpet |
| 00268757 | Clarinet | 00268760 | Trombone |
| 00268758 | Alto Sax | | |

## Billie Eilish
9 songs
| | | | |
|---|---|---|---|
| 00345648 | Flute | 00345653 | Horn |
| 00345649 | Clarinet | 00345654 | Trombone |
| 00345650 | Alto Sax | 00345655 | Violin |
| 00345651 | Tenor Sax | 00345656 | Viola |
| 00345652 | Trumpet | 00345657 | Cello |

## Favorite Movie Themes
13 songs
| | | | |
|---|---|---|---|
| 00841166 | Flute | 00841168 | Trumpet |
| 00841167 | Clarinet | 00841170 | Trombone |
| 00841169 | Alto Sax | 00841296 | Violin |

## Gospel Hymns
15 songs
| | | | |
|---|---|---|---|
| 00194648 | Flute | 00194654 | Trombone |
| 00194649 | Clarinet | 00194655 | Violin |
| 00194650 | Alto Sax | 00194656 | Viola |
| 00194651 | Tenor Sax | 00194657 | Cello |
| 00194652 | Trumpet | | |

## Great Classical Themes
15 songs
| | | | |
|---|---|---|---|
| 00292727 | Flute | 00292733 | Horn |
| 00292728 | Clarinet | 00292735 | Trombone |
| 00292729 | Alto Sax | 00292736 | Violin |
| 00292730 | Tenor Sax | 00292737 | Viola |
| 00292732 | Trumpet | 00292738 | Cello |

## The Greatest Showman
8 songs
| | | | |
|---|---|---|---|
| 00277389 | Flute | 00277394 | Horn |
| 00277390 | Clarinet | 00277395 | Trombone |
| 00277391 | Alto Sax | 00277396 | Violin |
| 00277392 | Tenor Sax | 00277397 | Viola |
| 00277393 | Trumpet | 00277398 | Cello |

## Irish Favorites
31 songs
| | | | |
|---|---|---|---|
| 00842489 | Flute | 00842495 | Trombone |
| 00842490 | Clarinet | 00842496 | Violin |
| 00842491 | Alto Sax | 00842497 | Viola |
| 00842493 | Trumpet | 00842498 | Cello |
| 00842494 | Horn | | |

## Michael Jackson
11 songs
| | | | |
|---|---|---|---|
| 00119495 | Flute | 00119499 | Trumpet |
| 00119496 | Clarinet | 00119501 | Trombone |
| 00119497 | Alto Sax | 00119503 | Violin |
| 00119498 | Tenor Sax | 00119502 | Accomp. |

## Jazz & Blues
14 songs
| | | | |
|---|---|---|---|
| 00841438 | Flute | 00841441 | Trumpet |
| 00841439 | Clarinet | 00841443 | Trombone |
| 00841440 | Alto Sax | 00841444 | Violin |
| 00841442 | Tenor Sax | | |

## Jazz Classics
12 songs
| | | | |
|---|---|---|---|
| 00151812 | Flute | 00151816 | Trumpet |
| 00151813 | Clarinet | 00151818 | Trombone |
| 00151814 | Alto Sax | 00151819 | Violin |
| 00151815 | Tenor Sax | 00151821 | Cello |

## Les Misérables
13 songs
| | | | |
|---|---|---|---|
| 00842292 | Flute | 00842297 | Horn |
| 00842293 | Clarinet | 00842298 | Trombone |
| 00842294 | Alto Sax | 00842299 | Violin |
| 00842295 | Tenor Sax | 00842300 | Viola |
| 00842296 | Trumpet | 00842301 | Cello |

## Metallica
12 songs
| | | | |
|---|---|---|---|
| 02501327 | Flute | 02502454 | Horn |
| 02501339 | Clarinet | 02501329 | Trombone |
| 02501332 | Alto Sax | 02501334 | Violin |
| 02501333 | Tenor Sax | 02501335 | Viola |
| 02501330 | Trumpet | 02501338 | Cello |

## Motown Classics
15 songs
| | | | |
|---|---|---|---|
| 00842572 | Flute | 00842576 | Trumpet |
| 00842573 | Clarinet | 00842578 | Trombone |
| 00842574 | Alto Sax | 00842579 | Violin |
| 00842575 | Tenor Sax | | |

## Pirates of the Caribbean
16 songs
| | | | |
|---|---|---|---|
| 00842183 | Flute | 00842188 | Horn |
| 00842184 | Clarinet | 00842189 | Trombone |
| 00842185 | Alto Sax | 00842190 | Violin |
| 00842186 | Tenor Sax | 00842191 | Viola |
| 00842187 | Trumpet | 00842192 | Cello |

## Queen
17 songs
| | | | |
|---|---|---|---|
| 00285402 | Flute | 00285407 | Horn |
| 00285403 | Clarinet | 00285408 | Trombone |
| 00285404 | Alto Sax | 00285409 | Violin |
| 00285405 | Tenor Sax | 00285410 | Viola |
| 00285406 | Trumpet | 00285411 | Cello |

## Simple Songs
14 songs
| | | | |
|---|---|---|---|
| 00249081 | Flute | 00249087 | Horn |
| 00249093 | Oboe | 00249089 | Trombone |
| 00249082 | Clarinet | 00249090 | Violin |
| 00249083 | Alto Sax | 00249091 | Viola |
| 00249084 | Tenor Sax | 00249092 | Cello |
| 00249086 | Trumpet | 00249094 | Mallets |

## Superhero Themes
14 songs
| | | | |
|---|---|---|---|
| 00363195 | Flute | 00363200 | Horn |
| 00363196 | Clarinet | 00363201 | Trombone |
| 00363197 | Alto Sax | 00363202 | Violin |
| 00363198 | Tenor Sax | 00363203 | Viola |
| 00363199 | Trumpet | 00363204 | Cello |

## Star Wars
16 songs
| | | | |
|---|---|---|---|
| 00350900 | Flute | 00350907 | Horn |
| 00350913 | Oboe | 00350908 | Trombone |
| 00350903 | Clarinet | 00350909 | Violin |
| 00350904 | Alto Sax | 00350910 | Viola |
| 00350905 | Tenor Sax | 00350911 | Cello |
| 00350906 | Trumpet | 00350914 | Mallet |

## Taylor Swift
15 songs
| | | | |
|---|---|---|---|
| 00842532 | Flute | 00842537 | Horn |
| 00842533 | Clarinet | 00842538 | Trombone |
| 00842534 | Alto Sax | 00842539 | Violin |
| 00842535 | Tenor Sax | 00842540 | Viola |
| 00842536 | Trumpet | 00842541 | Cello |

## Video Game Music
13 songs
| | | | |
|---|---|---|---|
| 00283877 | Flute | 00283883 | Horn |
| 00283878 | Clarinet | 00283884 | Trombone |
| 00283879 | Alto Sax | 00283885 | Violin |
| 00283880 | Tenor Sax | 00283886 | Viola |
| 00283882 | Trumpet | 00283887 | Cello |

## Wicked
13 songs
| | | | |
|---|---|---|---|
| 00842236 | Flute | 00842241 | Horn |
| 00842237 | Clarinet | 00842242 | Trombone |
| 00842238 | Alto Sax | 00842243 | Violin |
| 00842239 | Tenor Sax | 00842244 | Viola |
| 00842240 | Trumpet | 00842245 | Cello |

*Prices, contents, and availability subject to change without notice.*

Disney characters and artwork ™ & © 2021 Disney

HAL•LEONARD®

# 101 SONGS

## BIG COLLECTIONS OF FAVORITE SONGS ARRANGED FOR SOLO INSTRUMENTALISTS.

## 101 BROADWAY SONGS

| | | |
|---|---|---|
| 00154199 | Flute | $15.99 |
| 00154200 | Clarinet | $15.99 |
| 00154201 | Alto Sax | $15.99 |
| 00154202 | Tenor Sax | $16.99 |
| 00154203 | Trumpet | $15.99 |
| 00154204 | Horn | $15.99 |
| 00154205 | Trombone | $15.99 |
| 00154206 | Violin | $15.99 |
| 0154207 | Viola | $15.99 |
| 0154208 | Cello | $15.99 |

## 101 DISNEY SONGS

| | | |
|---|---|---|
| 00244104 | Flute | $17.99 |
| 00244106 | Clarinet | $17.99 |
| 00244107 | Alto Sax | $17.99 |
| 00244108 | Tenor Sax | $17.99 |
| 00244109 | Trumpet | $17.99 |
| 00244112 | Horn | $17.99 |
| 00244120 | Trombone | $17.99 |
| 00244121 | Violin | $17.99 |
| 00244125 | Viola | $17.99 |
| 00244126 | Cello | $17.99 |

## 101 MOVIE HITS

| | | |
|---|---|---|
| 00158087 | Flute | $15.99 |
| 00158088 | Clarinet | $15.99 |
| 00158089 | Alto Sax | $15.99 |
| 00158090 | Tenor Sax | $15.99 |
| 00158091 | Trumpet | $15.99 |
| 00158092 | Horn | $15.99 |
| 00158093 | Trombone | $15.99 |
| 00158094 | Violin | $15.99 |
| 00158095 | Viola | $15.99 |
| 00158096 | Cello | $15.99 |

## 101 CHRISTMAS SONGS

| | | |
|---|---|---|
| 00278637 | Flute | $15.99 |
| 00278638 | Clarinet | $15.99 |
| 00278639 | Alto Sax | $15.99 |
| 00278640 | Tenor Sax | $15.99 |
| 00278641 | Trumpet | $15.99 |
| 00278642 | Horn | $14.99 |
| 00278643 | Trombone | $15.99 |
| 00278644 | Violin | $15.99 |
| 0278645 | Viola | $15.99 |
| 0278646 | Cello | $15.99 |

## 101 HIT SONGS

| | | |
|---|---|---|
| 00194561 | Flute | $17.99 |
| 00197182 | Clarinet | $17.99 |
| 00197183 | Alto Sax | $17.99 |
| 00197184 | Tenor Sax | $17.99 |
| 00197185 | Trumpet | $17.99 |
| 00197186 | Horn | $17.99 |
| 00197187 | Trombone | $17.99 |
| 00197188 | Violin | $17.99 |
| 00197189 | Viola | $17.99 |
| 00197190 | Cello | $17.99 |

## 101 POPULAR SONGS

| | | |
|---|---|---|
| 00224722 | Flute | $17.99 |
| 00224723 | Clarinet | $17.99 |
| 00224724 | Alto Sax | $17.99 |
| 00224725 | Tenor Sax | $17.99 |
| 00224726 | Trumpet | $17.99 |
| 00224727 | Horn | $17.99 |
| 00224728 | Trombone | $17.99 |
| 00224729 | Violin | $17.99 |
| 00224730 | Viola | $17.99 |
| 00224731 | Cello | $17.99 |

## 101 CLASSICAL THEMES

| | | |
|---|---|---|
| 00155315 | Flute | $15.99 |
| 00155317 | Clarinet | $15.99 |
| 00155318 | Alto Sax | $15.99 |
| 00155319 | Tenor Sax | $15.99 |
| 00155320 | Trumpet | $15.99 |
| 00155321 | Horn | $15.99 |
| 00155322 | Trombone | $15.99 |
| 00155323 | Violin | $15.99 |
| 0155324 | Viola | $15.99 |
| 0155325 | Cello | $15.99 |

## 101 JAZZ SONGS

| | | |
|---|---|---|
| 00146363 | Flute | $15.99 |
| 00146364 | Clarinet | $15.99 |
| 00146366 | Alto Sax | $15.99 |
| 00146367 | Tenor Sax | $15.99 |
| 00146368 | Trumpet | $15.99 |
| 00146369 | Horn | $14.99 |
| 00146370 | Trombone | $15.99 |
| 00146371 | Violin | $15.99 |
| 00146372 | Viola | $15.99 |
| 00146373 | Cello | $15.99 |

## 101 MOST BEAUTIFUL SONGS

| | | |
|---|---|---|
| 00291023 | Flute | $16.99 |
| 00291041 | Clarinet | $16.99 |
| 00291042 | Alto Sax | $17.99 |
| 00291043 | Tenor Sax | $17.99 |
| 00291044 | Trumpet | $16.99 |
| 00291045 | Horn | $16.99 |
| 00291046 | Trombone | $16.99 |
| 00291047 | Violin | $16.99 |
| 00291048 | Viola | $16.99 |
| 00291049 | Cello | $17.99 |

*See complete song lists and sample pages at www.halleonard.com*

### HAL•LEONARD®
www.halleonard.com

*Prices, contents and availability subject to change without notice.*